BRUNO LOUBET

Chicken

Photography by SIMON WHEELER

THE MASTER CHEFS

TED SMART

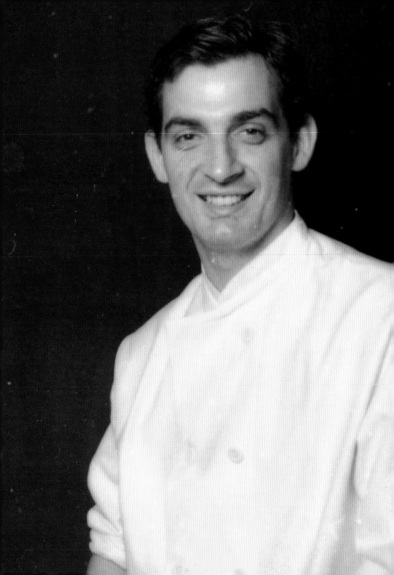

BRUNO LOUBET was born in the Bordeaux region of southwestern France. After working in restaurants in Brussels and Paris, Bruno came to London and worked for Pierre Koffman at La Tante Claire, before becoming head chef at a restaurant called Gastronome One, where he was awarded the title Young Chef of the Year 1985 by *The Good Food Guide*. After a spell with Raymond Blanc at Le Manoir Aux Quat'Saisons near Oxford, Bruno returned to London, to the Four Seasons at the Inn on the Park Hotel, where within one year he had earned his first Michelin star at the age of 29. He also found time to complete *Cuisine Courante* (Pavilion, 1992).

In 1992 Bruno opened Bistrot Bruno in London's Soho, which was named Restaurant of the Year 1994 by *The Times* and was given special awards in the 1994 *Michelin Guide* and Fay Maschler's *Evening Standard Restaurant Guide*. With the opening of his new restaurant, L'Odéon, in late 1995, he has appeared in *Vogue*, *Harper's & Queen* and numerous other magazines and newspapers. Bruno has also published a second book of recipes, *Bistrot Bruno: Cooking From L'Odéon* (Macmillan, 1995).

CONTENTS

Poultry is to the chef what

the canvas is to the artist.

INTRODUCTION

There are many reasons why the consumption of free-range poultry is increasing rapidly and people are looking for ways to make the most of the true flavours of chicken.

A technically complicated recipe with a lot of ingredients may not be the most enjoyable dish and, in my opinion, two or three flavours perfectly complementing each other are the best representation of good taste. In this book I have collected ten chicken recipes that I cook at home, and sometimes put on my lunch menu at L'Odéon.

To choose a good chicken, look for 'Free Range' (touch the back: it should be quite hard, proving the chicken 'has lived a bit'; if it feels soft the chicken has been force-fed to get bigger quickly – the flavour will be non-existent and the texture spongy) or maybe a French 'Label Rouge' chicken, a label of approved quality. I cannot wait for the day that England has an equivalent, as Scotland does with the Tartan Mark for salmon. This way we can all feel confident in the level of quality we are buying!

GRILLED CHICKEN ESCALOPES
and raw artichoke salad

2 GLOBE ARTICHOKES

½ A LEMON

85 G/3 OZ PARMESAN CHEESE

2 CHICKEN BREASTS, SKINNED AND
EACH OPENED OUT FLAT
('BUTTERFLIED') TO FORM
FOUR ESCALOPES

100 ML/3½ FL OZ VIRGIN OLIVE OIL

SALT AND PEPPER

2 TABLESPOONS FINELY CHOPPED
FRESH PARSLEY

25 G/1 OZ PINE KERNELS, TOASTED

SERVES 4

Snap off all the coarse outside leaves from the artichokes. Using a stainless steel knife, gently remove all the green leaves, the cone of pointed violet leaves and finally the hairy choke. Put 300 ml/½ pint water in a small bowl. Squeeze the lemon into the water, add the squeezed half lemon and immerse the artichokes in the lemon water. Cover with clingfilm.

With a vegetable peeler, 'shave' the Parmesan on to a plate.

Brush the chicken escalopes with olive oil, season with salt and pepper then char-grill on a hot cast-iron ridged grill pan or under a very hot grill; it will take only a few minutes to cook the chicken.

To serve, drain the artichokes, pat dry, slice finely and arrange on four plates. Place the grilled chicken on top of the artichokes. Sprinkle with the shaved Parmesan and the parsley. Grind over some black pepper, drizzle with olive oil and scatter on the pine kernels.

CHICKEN AND CORN SOUP
with green peppercorns

50 G/2 OZ BUTTER

225 G/8 OZ LEEKS, WHITE PARTS
    ONLY, ROUGHLY CHOPPED

2 GARLIC CLOVES, CHOPPED

1 LITRE/1¾ PINTS CHICKEN STOCK
    (PAGE 28)

15 GREEN PEPPERCORNS

100 ML/3½ FL OZ DOUBLE CREAM

2 TABLESPOONS CHOPPED FRESH
    CHIVES

450 G/1 LB CANNED SWEETCORN,
    DRAINED

175 G/6 OZ COOKED CHICKEN
    BREAST, SKINNED AND DICED
    (OPTIONAL)

SALT AND PEPPER

SERVES 6

Melt the butter in a large
saucepan, add the chopped leeks
and garlic and cook gently, without
colouring, for about 5 minutes or
until the leeks soften slightly. Add
the stock, green peppercorns and
cream and simmer for 30 minutes.

Purée the soup in a liquidizer
or with a hand-blender. Strain into
a clean pan, bring to the boil and
then add the chives, the drained
sweetcorn and the diced chicken, if
using. Taste and adjust the
seasoning and serve hot.

*To achieve the cappuccino effect,
top the soup with milk froth, made
by bringing a saucepan of milk to
the boil and then blending with a
hand-blender until froth forms.*

CLAY POT SPICY CHICKEN

1 CINNAMON STICK

1 CHICKEN, ABOUT 1.8 KG/4 LB

½ A LEMON

SALT AND PEPPER

4 TABLESPOONS CLEAR HONEY

½ TABLESPOON CRUSHED
   CORIANDER SEEDS

4 GARLIC CLOVES, CRUSHED

½ TEASPOON CHOPPED, SEEDED
   FRESH RED CHILLI

1 TABLESPOON ROUGHLY CHOPPED
   FRESH MINT

½ A CHICKEN STOCK CUBE

4 TABLESPOONS RED WINE VINEGAR

2 TOMATOES, EACH CUT INTO FOUR

3 TABLESPOONS OLIVE OIL

1 TABLESPOON ROUGHLY CHOPPED
   FRESH FLAT-LEAF PARSLEY

SERVES 4

Soak the clay pot in water for 30 minutes. Preheat the oven to 180°C/350°F/Gas Mark 4.

Place the cinnamon stick inside the chicken. Rub the chicken all over with the lemon, season with salt and pepper, then place in the clay pot. Spread the chicken with the honey, then add all the other ingredients to the clay pot, except the parsley. Place the pot in the oven and bake for 45 minutes.

Open the pot and quickly sprinkle the parsley over the chicken, then close the pot again, re-opening at the table to release all the delightful spicy aromas.

Serve with mashed potato, to which you have added plenty of chopped spring onions.

COQ AU VIN

1 COCKEREL OR LARGE CHICKEN, ABOUT 2.5 KG/5½ LB, CUT INTO EIGHT PIECES

2 CARROTS, THICKLY SLICED

2 STICKS OF CELERY, THICKLY SLICED

2 ONIONS, ROUGHLY CHOPPED

4 GARLIC CLOVES, CRUSHED

1 BAY LEAF

1 SPRIG OF THYME

1.5 LITRES/2½ PINTS RED WINE

6 TABLESPOONS SEASONED FLOUR

4 TABLESPOONS OLIVE OIL

1 SPRIG OF TARRAGON

ABOUT 1 LITRE/1¾ PINTS VEAL STOCK

SALT AND PEPPER

100 G/3½ OZ STREAKY BACON, CUT INTO THICK STRIPS (LARDONS)

20 BUTTON ONIONS

125 G/4 OZ BUTTON MUSHROOMS

SERVES 4–6

Begin 3 days before serving. Put the chicken in a large bowl, add the carrots, celery, onions, garlic, bay leaf, thyme and wine. Mix, cover and refrigerate overnight.

The next day, drain the chicken and vegetables in a colander over a bowl to reserve the wine marinade.

Pat the chicken dry with paper towels, then toss in seasoned flour. Heat the oil in a frying pan and brown the chicken, then transfer to a flameproof casserole.

In the same frying pan, fry the carrots, onions and celery until well browned, then add the wine marinade and pour over the chicken, adding the garlic, bay leaf, thyme and tarragon. Bring to the boil, simmer for 10 minutes, then add enough veal stock to cover the chicken. Cover with a lid and simmer very gently for 1 hour.

Drain in a colander over a bowl, then pour the sauce into a pan and boil to reduce and thicken. Strain through a fine sieve into a clean saucepan. Season to taste, add the chicken and set aside.

Fry the bacon strips gently until golden. Add the button onions and fry until lightly coloured, then add to the sauce. In the same pan, sauté the mushrooms for a few minutes, then add to the sauce. Simmer for 15 minutes. Leave to cool, then cover with clingfilm and refrigerate for 48 hours (see page 30).

To serve, reheat and simmer for 5 minutes.

CHICKEN PASTILLA

4 CHICKEN THIGHS, SKINNED
5 TABLESPOONS OLIVE OIL
100 G/3½ OZ SHALLOTS, CHOPPED
1 SMALL AUBERGINE, FINELY DICED
¾ TEASPOON GROUND CORIANDER
3 PINCHES OF GROUND CINNAMON
LARGE PINCH OF SAFFRON
    STRANDS
85 G/3 OZ RAISINS, SOAKED
    OVERNIGHT IN WATER
1 GARLIC CLOVE, CHOPPED
1 TEASPOON CHOPPED FRESH
    THYME
1 TABLESPOON CHOPPED FRESH
    MINT
SALT AND PEPPER
16 ROUND SPRING ROLL WRAPPERS
1 EGG, BEATEN

SERVES 4

Fry the chicken in 1 tablespoon of the oil until cooked. Leave to cool.

Preheat the oven to 180°C/350°F/Gas Mark 4.

In a saucepan heat 3 tablespoons of the olive oil and cook the shallots until soft. Add the diced aubergine, stir well, then add the coriander, cinnamon, saffron, raisins, garlic and thyme. Cook over a very low heat for 10 minutes, then turn off the heat and add the mint.

Cut the chicken into fine strips and add to the aubergine mixture. Stir to mix and season to taste.

Brush eight of the spring roll wrappers with beaten egg, then lay the other eight wrappers on top of them. Divide the chicken mixture between four of the doubled wrappers. Brush the edges with beaten egg and cover with the four remaining doubled wrappers. Press around the edges to seal, making four 'flying saucer' shaped pastillas. Brush both sides of each pastilla with the remaining olive oil.

Place the pastillas on a baking sheet and bake for about 8 minutes or until golden brown and crisp.

PANCETTA-WRAPPED CHICKEN
with asparagus and hazelnut risotto

4 CHICKEN BREASTS, SKINNED
SALT AND PEPPER
12 THIN SLICES OF PANCETTA
1 TABLESPOON OLIVE OIL
50 G/2 OZ BUTTER
2 SMALL ONIONS, FINELY CHOPPED
2 GARLIC CLOVES, FINELY CHOPPED
350 G/13 OZ RISOTTO RICE
½ A GLASS OF DRY WHITE WINE
900 ML/1½ PINTS CHICKEN STOCK
    (PAGE 28), HOT
450 G/1 LB GREEN ASPARAGUS,
    PEELED
2 TABLESPOONS FRESHLY GRATED
    PARMESAN CHEESE
2 TABLESPOONS CHOPPED FRESH
    CHERVIL
85 G/3 OZ HAZELNUTS, TOASTED

SERVES 4

Season the chicken with salt and pepper and wrap each breast in three slices of pancetta. Heat the oil in a heavy-based frying pan, add the chicken and fry until lightly and evenly browned, then lower the heat and cook slowly for about 7–8 minutes on each side. When the chicken is cooked, cover the pan with foil and set aside.

Melt the butter in a wide, heavy saucepan, add the onions and garlic and cook until the onions are soft, stirring occasionally. Add the rice and stir well to coat the grains with the butter. Add the wine and simmer until absorbed by the rice, stirring constantly.

Add a small ladleful of hot stock and stir well all around the pan and across the bottom to ensure that the rice does not stick. Cook, stirring constantly, until the stock has been absorbed, then repeat the process until all the stock has been used and the rice is just tender to the bite, about 20 minutes. If the rice needs further cooking, add a little boiling water and keep stirring.

Meanwhile, blanch the asparagus in salted boiling water, drain and cut into 2.5 cm/1 inch pieces. Add the asparagus to the risotto and stir in the Parmesan. Season to taste, then add the chervil and the hazelnuts. Spoon on to deep plates and arrange the chicken on top. Sprinkle with a few drops of olive oil and some freshly ground pepper.

CHICKEN IN A SALT CRUST

1 CHICKEN, ABOUT 1.8 KG/4 LB
2 TABLESPOONS OLIVE OIL
FRESHLY GROUND BLACK PEPPER
FEW SPRIGS OF FRESH ROSEMARY
FEW SPRIGS OF FRESH MARJORAM
  (OPTIONAL)
1 EGG YOLK, BEATEN WITH
  1 TABLESPOON WATER

SALT CRUST
1 KG/2¼ LB PLAIN FLOUR
6 EGG WHITES
500 G/1 LB 2 OZ SALT

SAUCE
100 G/3½ OZ BUTTER
4 TABLESPOONS WORCESTERSHIRE
  SAUCE
100 ML/3½ FL OZ CHICKEN STOCK
  OR WATER
1 TABLESPOON CHOPPED FRESH
  LOVAGE
½ A LEMON

SERVES 4–6

To make the crust, place the flour, egg whites and salt in a large bowl and beat with an electric mixer on medium speed for 1 minute. Add just enough water to bind to a dough. Shape into a ball.

Preheat the oven to 150°C/300°F/Gas Mark 2. Brush the chicken with oil; season with pepper.

On a lightly floured surface, roll out the salt dough to an oblong about 8 mm/⅜ inch thick; it should be large enough to wrap comfortably around the chicken.

Make a bed of herbs on one side of the salt dough and set the chicken on top. Brush the dough around the chicken with the egg wash. Place more herbs over the chicken, then roll it over to wrap it in the salt dough. Seal all the joins completely with the egg wash, pressing with your fingers. Place, seam down, on a baking sheet and bake for 1¼ hours.

Remove from the oven and leave to rest for 15 minutes.

Meanwhile, make the sauce: melt the butter in a saucepan and heat until it turns a hazelnut colour. Remove from the heat and stir in the Worcestershire sauce, stock or water and lovage. Add a squeeze of lemon juice. Keep warm.

Take the chicken to the table in its crust. Cut around the salt crust, lift off the top, then lift out the chicken, discard the herbs and carve the chicken.

CHICKEN À LA KIEV

100 G/3½ OZ BUTTER, AT ROOM
    TEMPERATURE
50 G/2 OZ FRESH FLAT-LEAF
    PARSLEY, FINELY CHOPPED
50 G/2 OZ FRESH TARRAGON,
    FINELY CHOPPED
50 G/2 OZ FRESH CHERVIL,
    FINELY CHOPPED
1 GARLIC CLOVE, CRUSHED, THEN
    FINELY CHOPPED
1 TABLESPOON WHOLEGRAIN
    MUSTARD
GRATED ZEST AND JUICE OF
    1 LEMON
1 TEASPOON PAPRIKA
SALT AND PEPPER
4 CHICKEN BREASTS, SKINNED
6 TABLESPOONS FLOUR
2 EGGS, BEATEN
10 TABLESPOONS FRESH WHITE
    BREADCRUMBS
VEGETABLE OIL FOR DEEP-FRYING

SERVES 4

Begin making this dish the day
before you want to serve it. Place
the butter in a bowl and mix in
the parsley, tarragon, chervil, garlic,
mustard, paprika, lemon zest and
juice; season with salt and pepper
and place in the refrigerator.

Cover the chicken breasts with
clingfilm and, using a rolling pin,
flatten each breast until it forms an
escalope or 'supreme' about
5 mm/¼ inch thick. Season with
salt and pepper, then place some of
the herb butter in the centre of
each breast. Roll up the breasts to
completely enclose the butter,
wrap each one separately in
clingfilm and place in the
refrigerator overnight.

To cook the chicken, place the
flour in a shallow dish, the well-
beaten eggs in a second dish and
the breadcrumbs in a third dish.
Heat the oil for deep-frying to
160°C/325°F.

Coat each chicken supreme
first in the flour, then in the egg
and finally in the breadcrumbs,
gently shaking off any excess.
Deep-fry the breasts for about
8 minutes, then drain on paper
towels to absorb any fat.

Serve with boiled or steamed
french beans, mangetout or
asparagus; the butter from the
chicken will act as a sauce.

BRUNO'S CHICKEN CURRY

3 TABLESPOONS VEGETABLE OIL

2 SMALL ONIONS

1 TABLESPOON CURRY MIX
(PAGE 29)

12 CHICKEN THIGHS, SKINNED AND
CUT INTO 2 CM/¾ INCH CUBES

4 GARLIC CLOVES, CHOPPED

¾ TEASPOON CHOPPED FRESH
GINGER

1 STALK OF LEMONGRASS, OUTER
PART REMOVED, HEART CHOPPED

½ CHICKEN STOCK CUBE

125 ML/4 FL OZ CARROT JUICE

125 ML/4 FL OZ APPLE JUICE

50 G/2 OZ CREAMED COCONUT
(FROM A BLOCK), DISSOLVED IN A
LITTLE BOILING WATER

SALT

SUGAR

2 RIPE TOMATOES, CUT INTO
1 CM/½ INCH CUBES

1 TABLESPOON CHOPPED FRESH
CORIANDER

100 G/3½ OZ NATURAL YOGURT

SERVES 4

Heat the oil in a heavy saucepan, then add the onions and the curry mix. Fry for a few minutes, stirring, until the onions soften and the spices are fragrant.

Add the chicken, garlic, ginger and lemongrass and crumble in the stock cube. Fry and stir for 2 minutes, then pour in the carrot and apple juices and the coconut cream. Season with salt and 3 pinches of sugar. Leave to simmer gently for 20 minutes.

Remove from the heat and add the tomatoes, coriander and yogurt. Stir well and serve hot, with plain boiled rice.

STUFFED CHICKEN LEG
with almond and lime pickle potatoes

4 TABLESPOONS OLIVE OIL

1 ONION, CHOPPED

85 G/3 OZ SUN-DRIED TOMATOES
IN OIL, DRAINED AND CHOPPED

2 GARLIC CLOVES, CHOPPED

1 TABLESPOON CHOPPED FRESH
CORIANDER

4 CHICKEN LEG JOINTS, BONED
(PAGE 30), BONES RESERVED

12 THIN SLICES OF PANCETTA

SAUCE

2 TABLESPOONS OLIVE OIL

3 SHALLOTS, CHOPPED

2 SMALL CARROTS, CHOPPED

1 STICK OF CELERY, CHOPPED

200 G/7 OZ RIPE TOMATOES,
SEEDED AND CHOPPED

100 ML/3½ FL OZ DRY WHITE WINE

1 GARLIC CLOVE, CHOPPED

500 ML/16 FL OZ CHICKEN STOCK
(PAGE 28), BOILED WITH
2–3 DROPS DARK SOY SAUCE
TO REDUCE TO 200 ML/7 FL OZ

40 G/1½ OZ BUTTER, DICED

SALT AND PEPPER

TO SERVE

ALMOND AND LIME PICKLE
POTATOES (PAGE 30)

SERVES 4

In a frying pan, heat 2 tablespoons of the olive oil and cook the onion until soft. Add the sun-dried tomatoes, garlic and coriander. Leave on a plate until cold.

Stuff the chicken legs with the tomato mixture. Wrap the legs in pancetta and tie with string. Refrigerate until ready to cook.

To make the sauce, heat the olive oil in a heavy-based saucepan, add the chicken bones and brown for a few minutes, then add the shallots, carrots and celery and cook, stirring, until the vegetables are turning golden. Add the tomatoes, wine and garlic and cook for a few minutes. Add the stock and simmer gently for 30 minutes.

Strain the sauce through a fine sieve into a clean saucepan. Bring back to the boil and whisk in the butter, a few pieces at a time. Season to taste. Keep warm.

Fry the chicken legs in the remaining oil in a covered pan for about 10 minutes, turning from time to time. Remove the string and cut each leg into three. Serve with the sauce and potatoes.

THE BASICS

WHITE CHICKEN STOCK

450 G/1 LB CHICKEN WINGS

SALT

1 ONION, CHOPPED

2 GARLIC CLOVES

2 STICKS OF CELERY, CHOPPED

½ A BAY LEAF

1 SPRIG OF THYME

MAKES 1.5 LITRES/2½ PINTS

Place the chicken wings in a heavy saucepan with 2 litres/3½ pints water and a pinch of salt. Bring to the boil, then skim the surface. Add the remaining ingredients and simmer gently for 1 hour.

Pour into a colander over a bowl, then strain through a fine sieve into a clean saucepan. Bring to the boil and boil until reduced to 1.5 litres/2½ pints.

Freeze in three containers, so you have 500 ml/16 fl oz portions to use as required.

CURRY MIX

3 TABLESPOONS CORIANDER SEEDS
8 GREEN CARDAMOM PODS,
   CRUSHED AND BITS OF PODS
   REMOVED
1 BLACK CARDAMOM POD, CRUSHED
   AND BITS OF POD REMOVED
1 TEASPOON CUMIN SEEDS
1 TEASPOON FENUGREEK SEEDS
2 WHOLE CLOVES
2 TABLESPOONS WHITE MUSTARD
   SEEDS
1 TEASPOON WHITE PEPPERCORNS
2 TABLESPOONS TURMERIC
1 BAY LEAF
¼ TEASPOON DRIED HOT PEPPER
   FLAKES
¼ TEASPOON DRIED GARLIC OR
   GARLIC POWDER

Put the coriander seeds, cardamom seeds, cumin seeds, fenugreek seeds, cloves, mustard seeds and peppercorns in a small frying pan and heat gently for 5 minutes, stirring constantly until the spices are very aromatic.

Remove from the heat and add all remaining ingredients.

Work the mixture to a powder in a spice mill, coffee grinder or mortar and pestle. Store in an airtight jar.

ALMOND AND LIME PICKLE POTATOES

450 G/1 LB NEW POTATOES
2 TABLESPOONS SUNFLOWER OIL
50 G/2 OZ ALMONDS, TOASTED
½ TABLESPOON FINELY CHOPPED
   LIME PICKLE
½ TABLESPOON CHOPPED FRESH
   CORIANDER
½ A LEMON

SERVES 4

Boil the potatoes, peel and trim to even barrel shapes if you like. Heat the oil in a frying pan and sauté the boiled potatoes until they are golden brown.

Add the almonds and chopped lime pickle and toss for 1 minute, then add the coriander and serve at once.

TIPS AND TECHNIQUES

STEWS AND CASSEROLES

To really intensify and improve the flavour and depth of the sauce, make your stew 2 or 3 days before you want to serve it. Every day, reheat the stew gently and simmer for 5 minutes, then leave to cool and place in the refrigerator. This technique is applicable to any stew.

BONING CHICKEN LEGS

Chicken legs are elevated to the same status usually reserved for breasts if they are boned and stuffed. This also makes them quicker to cook and easier to eat. Slide a long, thin, sharp knife all around the bone, without cutting through the skin. Ease the bones out and reserve to make a sauce or stock.

THE MASTER CHEFS

THE MASTER CHEFS

This edition produced for The Book People Ltd,

Hall Wood Avenue, Haydock, St Helens WAII 9UL

Photographs © copyright 1996 Simon Wheeler

First published in 1996 by

WEIDENFELD & NICOLSON

THE ORION PUBLISHING GROUP

ORION HOUSE

5 UPPER ST MARTIN'S LANE

LONDON WC2H 9EA

British Library Cataloguing-in-Publication data
A catalogue record for this book is available
from the British Library.

ISBN 0 297 82179 2

DESIGNED BY THE SENATE

EDITOR MAGGIE RAMSAY

FOOD STYLIST JOY DAVIES

ASSISTANT KATY HOLDER